MODELING
AS YOUR JOB

MODELING AS YOUR JOB

A STEP BY STEP GUIDE ON HOW YOU CAN BECOME A WORKING MODEL

REVIVED

PJ Medina

authorHOUSE®

AuthorHouse™
1663 Liberty Drive
Bloomington, IN 47403
www.authorhouse.com
Phone: 1-800-839-8640

© 2005, 2013 by PJ Medina. All rights reserved.

No part of this book may be reproduced, stored in a retrieval system, or transmitted by any means without the written permission of the author.

Published by AuthorHouse   01/18/2013

ISBN: 978-1-4817-0868-5 (hc)
ISBN: 978-1-4817-0869-2 (e)

Library of Congress Control Number: 2013901135

Any people depicted in stock imagery provided by Thinkstock are models, and such images are being used for illustrative purposes only.
Certain stock imagery © Thinkstock.

This book is printed on acid-free paper.

Because of the dynamic nature of the Internet, any web addresses or links contained in this book may have changed since publication and may no longer be valid. The views expressed in this work are solely those of the author and do not necessarily reflect the views of the publisher, and the publisher hereby disclaims any responsibility for them.

ACKNOWLEDGMENT

I want to start by thanking Jesus the Christ for rising from death to give me the forgiveness of my sins and the power of the Holy Spirit to live new lives for the Father's glory.

I would like to take the time to thank some very important people in my life to start with: Maria t Gonzalez (mom) for standing by me, supporting me through the bad times, and boy there were some bad ones!

I love you.

To Wilma medina (mima) for all you has done for me and always without judgment.

To DR. Nathaniel Bent-Shaw for being they're to pick me up I thank you. There are so many people to whom I am indebted and to whom I wish to express my gratitude. Thank you Sammy medina, Porfirio medina (papi) Comair Months, Colin Anima, Kathryn Manning.

I want acknowledge two very important individuals who have been with me by my side and never stopped believing in me and in this journey Joseph Montalvo and Damian Contreras I shall always be indebted to you guys.

Michelle Rodriguez Lara for making sure it all makes sense I love you.

PJ Medina

And lastly, I would like to give a special thank-you to all who made *MODELING AS YOUR Job* possible.

I am aware that gratitude is the greatest amplifier of life; I say to you I am truly GRATEFUL to you for purchasing this book.

AUTHOR'S NOTES

It is my beliefs that the As Your Job brand is in no question the best how-to series of publications in the market place today. No other publication can match this level of success that the AS YOUR JOB can.

And here is the reason why. Only the AS YOUR JOB publication focuses on not only the fundamentals but also on what should a person be thinking, doing, and that person's personal finances. Putting it together in a simple to read step-by-step process that anyone can understand. The AS YOUR JOB publication literally takes the person by the hand and step-by-step walks them though the process.

No other publication can collapse the time frame it takes a person to for fill their dreams, like the AS YOUR JOB can. This series points out all the common mistakes and pitfalls and show you the reader a clear path.

This is why I am so proud of the AS YOUR JOB book series and if you're like me and like this book why not tell someone else, tell a friend or two.

Also available are:

Modeling As Your Job
Acting As Your Job

Coming soon:

Recording Artist As Your Job
Personal Trainer As Your Job

And more to come.

How to get the most out of this book

In this book we ARE NOT just addressing the business of MODELING, WE are ADDRESSING what you should be thinking, eating, and DOING, THE things you need BE CAREFUL OF, AND the steps you should BE TAKING in order to be SUCCESSFUL IN your quest of becoming a working MODEL. WITH that in mind, the book is broken down into steps you need to take baby step it IS A lot of information to take in. you should read each step APPLIES WHAT you've LEARNED, AND THEN move on to the next step. EACH STEP will bring you closer FOR FILLING your DREAM. in the book each step is broken down into departments they ARE:

MINDSET & TIME MANAGEMENT; IN this department YOU wiLL LEARN what you should be thinking, being a goal setter and a goal hitter

THE BUSINESS; IN this department you will learn the fundamentals of the modeling WORLD AS well AS THE how to

HEALTH & WELLNESS; IN this department you will learn how to take care OF THE PRODUCT (yourself.)

YOU'RE MONEY; IN this department you will learn how to manage your funds as well AS THE SCAMMER OUT there.

INTRODUCTION

My mission statement is to inspire others to live out their dreams; To be, do, and have anything that brings them joy, love, and happiness.

Living in New York, the city of dreams for most actors and models. I've have had the pleasure of meeting COUNTLESS MODELS and Actors. Who Struggle in the business, making one mistake after another while trying to be successful. And what I've Found is that they all make the same mistake, but because of lack of information or very little of it they don't become as successful as they should most just give up the Dream.

One day while talking with a friend who was starting a modeling career, ASKED, "HOW should I STARTS?" I told him what little I knew, it turnout what little I knew to him, was a lot of information. To which he replayed "IF you know so much why don't you MANAGE MY career?" I can not manage YOU; YOU have to manage yourself" I replied.

The idea for this book was born. After one year of research and interviewing dozens of Models, actors and doing countless hours of research, the book was completed. Now the mission of this book is to give the average person the tools, contacts and common pitfalls of the modeling industry. So that he or she can for fill their dream of becoming a working model or actor.

You must understand that the information in this book REPRESENT MY VIEWS and opinions and is INTENDED as information, not a guarantee of results there is many factors that must be CONSIDERED.

As with everything in life there are no guarantees.

However you must believe me when I tell you, you can be, do, have anything you dream of and I mean anything.

What I want you to understand is that their are three basic things that prevent a person for living out they dream of becoming a working model, and those three things are, one the way they think, two the business aspect of it and three their finance.

Let me explain what I mean by this statement.

One, when I talk about the mind or the mindset what I am referring to is what is knows as internal dialogue. The things you tell yourself when you're by yourself or the thoughts in your head, maybe you may want to call it the little voice in your head. I'm too fat, I'm too short, I'm not good looking enough, I'm too dark or I'm too pale white.

I don't know what I'm doing, whatever the case maybe you get my point.

It's really about controlling the way you think and controlling what you should be focused on. We are the one's who create the obstacles they do not exist. We create them and because we create them they become real to us.

But if you believe in yourself and believe in what you can create, nothing can stop you. You will move mountains.

The second thing that stops a person is the business they have no clue how to be an model. What it in tales, what steps need to be taken, what education is needed, you don't even know how to get started. You don't know these things so they become obstacles.

The third thing is the finance, the money.

You don't have the money to support yourself while going to go and see to become a model or how will you buy food and pay rent? Where will you find the resources to keep you afloat till you get your big break? You don't even know,

What you don't know!

And let's not forget all your friend and family members telling you, you'll never make it, give it up your a dreamer. Wake up and smell the coffee. Go get a real job you loser!

All these things now feed into the mindset then you start to tell yourself, you see I knew I couldn't do it. Do not believe any of it, it's a lie. What I'm going to cover in this book are these three things so that you have the tools, and have a fighting chance.

The way I'm going to do this is to address these three things in a step-by-step format. For A total of seven steps, Lucky seven

What I'm saying to you is follow these seven steps one by one and apply the principles in this book and by the time you have completed the seventh step you will be a model. Instead of chapters you and I will be taking steps.

My recommendation is to read the entire book the first time around then re-read the book starting with step one. Work your way down applying what your have learned and following each step. Do not skip steps, read the step apply it, and then move on to the next step!

Step-by-step you will fulfill your dream of becoming a working model.

It bears repeating:

My mission statement is to inspire others to live out their dreams; To be, do, and have anything that brings them joy, love, and happiness. This is my sincere desire for you.

I promise it will not be easy, but it will be worth it.

STEP ONE

MINDSET

STEP ONE

Mindset

YOU ARE A BUSINESS OWNER.

Modeling is a business it's your business you are the owner you work for yourself but not by yourself. Like a business owner you have great responsibility, but with great responsibility comes great reward. You are the boss. It starts and ends with you.

Here is some food for thought. I read this some time ago.

In the plans of the savanna every morning a lion wakes up knowing that today he must outrun the fastest gazelle or he will starve. Every morning a gazelle awakes knowing that today he must outrun the fastest lion or he will not survive. Every morning both must awake ready to run. The same applies to you wake up every morning ready to run.

Modeling is a world of egos with that said you the model must have great self-esteem because someone will always try to tare you down.

Fact 2 out of 3 American has low self-esteem.

But where does someone get great self-esteem or maintain theirs? To answer this, one must first understand where it comes from. It comes from our childhood and it starts with your parents. It is the things we are told as children that mold our self-esteem as well as things we believe. Things Like you are to short, to fat, or ugly. But the good news is that self-esteem is like gold when it's hard it's beautiful and it latest forever. Everyone wants it everyone wants to show it off but more importantly it can be molded and molded into whatever you want it to be. The ideas and ways model think can be learned there is no one that can learn the natural skills the supermodel has to be successful. What makes a supermodel a supermodel is that he or she was trained to be successful, and so can you. We are going to teach you those same skills here.

But you must take action; the things you learn here are of no use if you do not take action. Action is what separates the working model from the want to be model. Let me ask you this; do you think a person can learn how to swim in a classroom? No you have got to jump in the water and move your hands, arm, and feet. You can read all the books in the world but you have got to act. You have to get out there and go for it just do it over and over again till the job gets done. Life rewards action so close your eyes and jump in. Odds are 1 out of 50 will make it big in modeling because of not caring of what people think they're just doing what needs to be done. The most important action a model can take is asking for what he or she wants.

STEP ONE

Mindset

TIME MANAGEMENT THE ABILITY TO MANAGE YOURSELF.

Time management your ability to manage your time will determine how successful you become. Managing your time will help you become more disciplined. You must plan your day, get a planning system, ether a day timer or an "at a glance planner". You should never go anywhere without your planner because everything should be in there.

Everything has to go in your day planner if you make a promise to someone its in your planner, If you have a booking, its in your planner do not put it anywhere else because all you have to do at the end of your day is look at your planner and there it is. You do not have to worry. And if you follow your planner you will get it all done write ever, single thing down!

Have a system of task completion; after you complete a task check it off. You have got it done and you do not have to think about it.

<u>If you lack discipline with your time you have little or no chance of being successful</u>.

Your ability to manage your time and yourself will determine how successful you will become as a model.

PJ Medina

Your going to need to bulletproof yourself and put yourself in a bubble that nothing can penetrate.

In this book I will give you the tools you are going to need to remain focused on the goal of become not just a model but also a working model.

Hollywood and New York City are filled with models, but few of them are working and that is the reason I wrote this book to produce working model.

Ok here we go lets talk about the topic of time management in my opinion the second most important aspect to your success or failure. You're going to need a system of task completion, like a To Do List, using a smart phone, daily planner or tablet. Whatever you choose, your going to write every task down and Trust me you think you can remember everything but you can't so write everything down.

Now at night before your head hits the pillow your going to write down the six most important things you need to get done the following day and your going to do this every night and your going to see to it that it gets done the following day. If you follow your planner you will get everything done, just check it off as it gets done then move on to the next task and one by one you'll get it all done you'll remain on task, you'll remain focused you will be successful. Your going to do this till your can afford to employee someone to do this for you, also known as personal assistant till then write it down, get it done.

One of the things I want to highlight is what I like to call winning the battle but losing the war and let me explain what I mean by this.

Sometimes we work so hard trying to land a gig, lets say a spot in a television show and it's a guest spot. We spend so must time celebrating, and rightfully you should that within six months to a year we're out of a job and out of money.

I'm not saying don't celebrate what I am saying is you must continue doing the things that got you the gig in the first place don't act as if you have arrived. Continue to look for work. Remember as an actor, your job is getting auditions and auditioning. Every time you land an audition, you are putting in a day of work. And always be on time! The worst thing you can do is being late.

Casting directors hate that not to say it costs them money. You want to see how fast you can get black listed just show up late.

STEP ONE

Mindset

GETTING DOWN TO THE FUNDAMENTALS OF THE BUSINESS, I MEAN THE MODELING BUSINESS.

Now as an model I think the first thing you should understand is the language. For this reason the glossary is first, call me crazy. How can you and I talk about building your business and becoming a working actor if you don't understand what I'm talking about?

Here are just some words and phrases that you need to know so that we can move faster.

AGENT—A person in an agency who finds people who have the potential to be successful models, signs a contract to represent them and to guide there careers

BODY SHOT—A picture of a in a bathing suit that shows her body from head to toe

BOOKERS—Refers to the person in an agency, who develops you as a model, books you for a job and oversees your career.

BOOKING—any job a model is hired to do.

CALL TIME—the time a model is expected to arrive at the job

CALL BACK—when an agency or client asks you to come back for a second interview

CASTING—Another word for goes and sees

COLLECTIONS—Refers to the collective showing of designer's new fashion in one particular city

COMMERCIAL AGENT—Handles models who don't fall into the traditional

COMMERCIAL MODEL—Models whom work primarily in local and secondary markets and appear mainly in catalogs and advertisements

CONTACT SHEET—a large sheet of photographic paper that has mini prints of all the pictures that were captured on one roll of film

COVER TRY—a photo shoot that's done to get a picture that's good enough to appear on a magazine cover

DAY RATE—The amount of money a model earns for a full day of work

EDITORIAL—Refers to any work that will appear in a magazine

FASHION CREDITS—In return for being allowed to borrow clothes from designers for fashions shoots; a magazine will identify the designer

FASHION SPREAD—a story spotlighting a particular fashion trend

FEATURED MODEL—The first or last model to appear in a runway show

GO AND SEE—An interview for a modeling job

IMAGE MODEL—Models who are new less than five years in the business

LOOK BOOKS—Photo albums put together by clothing companies so consumers can look at that season's styles

MEET AND GREET—a short interview that the judges and agents conduct with the participant at a model convention

MODEL EDITOR—Books all the models featured in a magazine

MOTHER AGENCY—The agency that discovered you, marketed you, and developed your career

OVEREXPOSED—a model is said to be overexposed when he or she has been working too much in one market

PORTFOLIO—An album of specially selected pictures you take to job interviews

PROFILE SHOT—a shot of the side of your face or body

READY TO WEAR—ready to wear clothes are mass produced

REAL PEOPLE MODELS—Represent all type of people. They appear mainly in ads and TV commercials

RUNWAY—also known as the catwalk a long narrow stage that juts out into the audience

SET—The area in a photo shoots where the pictures are actually taken

STRAIGHT ON SHOT—A photo in which your head and/or body are facing the camera

TENT—Short for tentative

TESTING PHOTOGRAPHERS—Photographers who do test shoots with aspiring models

THREE QUARTER ANGLE—In a photo you're facing slightly off to one side

WRAPPED—Means finished "were wrapped"

Before you move forward, make sure you know and understand these words and terms

By no means are we done I just wanted to scratched the surface of some of the words you will need to know and understand in order to moved forward. I think I hit some important ones.

STEP ONE

Modeling is a funny business it's the business of pretending

UNDERSTANDING YOUR BODY, HEALTH AND WELLNESS.

You as a model have to be aware of what you put into your body. It affects you`re energy, your skin, and let`s not forgets body fat.

Now as a model you must understand that it is not only about beauty but also about health and wellness. It is important that you the models know how to take care of yourself your physical appearance must always be at its best. Frequent haircuts, manicures, pedicures, facials and dental cleaning are vital and so is exercise.

Now I am are going to go over some simple tips to help lose the belly, love handles, and that gut if you have one. And define your abs. if you incorporate just a few into you lifestyle. You will find yourself with the belly you have always dreamed of.

- Do not skip meals. Not eating for long periods of time puts your body into a catabolic state. In other words your body starts to break down muscle tissue.
- Throw out your dinner plates. And buy smaller one. That way, even if you fill your plate you're eating a lot less.

- Avoid all foods that came from a box or bag. These foods are almost always highly processed carbs-foods that quickly raise blood-sugar levels and shut down the body's ability to burn fat.
- Have breakfast every morning. Research shows that obesity rates are lower in people who eat breakfast regularly, compared with people who don't. Research also showed that people getting calcium lose twice as much weight compared with people on low calcium diets. So load up on the yogurt.
- Avoid white bread people who eat white bread frequently weigh more than those who don't.
- Floss twice a day. Studies show that people with the highest level of inflammatory agents in their bodies were also the most likely to gain weight. Hate flossing studies also show that a dose of Listerine may be as effective at reducing levels of inflammatory bacteria within the mouth.

Skip on those potatoes. Any way you cook them; potato chips, mashed, or French. They raise levels of insulin in the blood, triggering your body to stop burning and start storing fat

You should focus on eating 5 to 6 small meals a day.

(Small being the key word) Below you will see a sample of 5 small meals on any given day.

Breakfast

Cereal with Banana Slices
1 cup (1oz) Multi-Grain Cereal
1 medium Banana
1/2 cup Skim Milk

PM Snack

Yogurt
6 oz Fat Free Yogurt

Lunch

Salad with Shredded Chicken
3 oz Shredded Chicken Breast, baked
1 Garden Salad w/ 2 tbs Fat Free Salad Dressing
1 small Whole Wheat Roll

PM Snack

Popcorn
3 cups Popcorn, Light or Air Popped

Dinner

Swordfish with Broccoli
4oz Swordfish, Grilled or Baked w/squeezed Lemon and Seasoning
1 cup Broccoli, Cooked
1/2 cup Brown Rice
1 Garden Salad w/ 2 tbs Fat Free Salad Dressing

Serving Size

Serving size information is important because the nutritional information provided is based on the serving size. For example, the serving size shown here is three cookies. If you consume six cookies, the nutritional values provided need to be doubled

Calories, Calories from Fat

The information in this section of the label helps you monitor the number of calories you take in each day. More importantly, it allows you to make healthy decisions about the foods you eat. Take a look at the number of calories from fat. In this example, 37% of the calories come from fat—anything over 30% is probably too much.

Total Fat, Saturated Fat

Try to choose products that are low in saturated fats and Trans fats, both of which are linked to an early onset of cardiovascular disease. Try to keep your consumption of saturated fat to less than 10% of your daily caloric intake

Cholesterol

Use this information to reduce the aging of your arteries. Limit your dietary cholesterol intake to less than 125 milligrams per 1,000 calories

Protein

You can get your protein from animal products, such as eggs, meat, or cheese, or from vegetable sources, such as soy products, nuts, legumes and beans, and seeds.

A diet high in vegetable proteins can help you live longer and younger. By themselves, the vegetable protein sources listed above contain less of a variety of amino acids (the building blocks of proteins) than meats, but when you combine these sources with whole grains such as brown rice, barley, and wheat, all your protein needs can be met.

Although it has not yet been determined scientifically how much protein you need every day, many experts suggest 15% to 20% of your daily calories should come from protein.

STEP ONE

Getting the job, getting the money, let the games begin

YOUR MONEY AND JOBS JUST FOR SURVIVAL.

Forming a plan

Nearly everyone has the ability to be successful, but very few have the desire and as the commitment to make the sacrifices necessary to achieve wealth.

1. Accept that you can achieve financial success and make a commitment to yourself to attain it. It is within your grasp if you really want it. Really BELIEVE it—that is the most important step. Only then will the incredible power of the human mind work out a means of achieving it. Reject the idea that work is simply something you have to do until the age of retirement.
2. Ask yourself this: Where do you want to be in 2,5,10 year's time? Set goals THAT EXCITES you. If you could do absolutely anything with your life, what would you DO? If you had unlimited money or found out you only had a month to live, what would you do? Write them down.
3. Establish your current financial position. What is the cash inflow and OUTFLOW? Horrors! Which areas can be improved upon? Everything!

4. Develop your NEW plans. Decide what action you are going to take that will move you closer to the achievement of your goals? All goals should be specific and have a time constraint.
5. Try to put extra savings into investment
6. Pursue your personal goals and business ideas with all you've got. With real PASSION and PURPOSE. If you really BELIEVE In them, they are far more likely to be achieved.
7. Still try to live a BALANCED life . . . or as balanced as you can make it. Money doesn't buy happiness; yet I'd rather be unhappy in comfort!
8. The highest cost of all is the cost of waiting to TAKE ACTION to change your current circumstances in life

STEP TWO

MODELING IS PUTTING ON THE BIGGEST FRONT

STEP TWO

Modeling is putting on the biggest front

CHANGING THE WAY YOU THINK.

Have you ever looked at a magazine advertisement and thought to you, "Wow if he or she can be a model so cans I?" Odds are you right. Have you ever hear the saying beauty is in the eyes of the beholder? You see modeling has more to do with health and energy and how you project that energy, than with beauty. If you think for a minute that you're not pretty enough or tall enough or super thin, we are here today to tell you. You are wrong. In today's crazy media world with advertiser competing for your dollars. Models are needed more than ever tall ones, short ones, and the boy next door, the crazy cool dude. You see advertisers need to move goods and services to the average consumer. Thus the average model is needed.

STEP TWO

Modeling is putting on the biggest front

TIME MANAGEMENT THE ABILITY TO MANAGE YOURSELF.

At this phase of this book I want to talk to you about purpose, because if you lack purpose you will not find the time or the ability to make the time to take classes, meet with an acting coach, get the training or find the school that you will need.

Without purpose you'll make excuses and justification as to the reason why you didn't take the classes or find the school or have the time. If you don't really know when you've met your purpose or when you're off track then your purpose is not clear enough. If you ask yourself the question when will I know if I'm off purpose? Must have a clear answer.

You must know, and be very clear as to the reason why you must master your craft and there must be clarity. Until you have a clear mind as to the reason why, you will not find the purpose for mastering your craft, you will never make the time to become a working actor. So right now find your purpose ask yourself what is the purpose for me to become a master at acting? And write it down and look at it everyday.

There must be some standards or principles you must uphold and there are going to be some thing you're going to have to give up in order to make the time to do what you have to do. You can not continue do the thing you have been doing or you will continue to have the things you have now, in other word, there are going to have to be some sacrifices, you must be will to pay in order to make the time you need to do what needs to get done. If not the result will be unproductive distraction and stress.

One of the things that you'll need to address is the organizing phase; this is the time that you put the sequences of events and or priorities what things must happen first. Like should you Google schools, or an acting coach or maybe figure out how will you pay for this or that, just get organized, and as always write it down, study it, think about it and plan it out.

Let me leave you with this final thought and just move on to the business aspect of step two. *It is my belief, that it is what you do when no one is around or looking that determines how successful and famous you become.*

STEP TWO

Where do you fit in?

GETTING DOWN TO THE FUNDAMENTALS OF THE BUSINESS, I MEAN MODELING BUSINESS.

New York City is the number one city for models. It is the heart of the fashion and advertising industries in the United States, which leads to a high demand for all types of models. The modeling agencies in New York compete to fill that demand with the finest talent in the nation. When an agency sees someone who has potential or someone who satisfies the demand, they will invest in that individual to get him or her ready for the market. They do not do this to be nice people—they do it because they feel they can make money from that person. They know the market and they will invest in you (a loan against future earnings) to prepare you for that market. If they guess wrong and you do not become marketable and profitable, they will cut their losses and drop you. The top agencies are working with big-budget ad agencies and fashion designers so there is money available to develop new talent. These top agencies will help train you (more like on the job training), get you test shoots, layout your portfolio, and put together comp cards and other printed materials you need. They take care of finding you work, booking the jobs, bill for the jobs and eventually cut a check for the work you do. Once you are in an agency like this all you have to worry about is following instructions and modeling.

In charge of developing you and booking all your jobs is the "new face" department of your agency. The Booker or manager this person in the agency that is responsible of developing you the model and booking jobs for you. He or she will also want to get your book or portfolio together by sending you to some reputable photographer who will take test pictures of you for this reason spending lots of money in test shoots before you land an agent are a waist. Your booker will choose the photo that will appear in your book and will arrange the order of your pictures in the book in a way that will sell you to the client.

From the new face dept, you the model will go to the management department, of the agency that will focus on expanding your look to see what type of client are interested in you and decide how you should focus your career and what you should do next.

All agencies have a department, that handles the supermodel or "next" supermodel so it handles image or the creation of a supermodel or cover girl.

At last there is the runway department this department handles runway booking for all the models in the agency. The runway department does all the necessary scheduling and negotiating for all the models. This department also handles models that mostly do runway shows or fitting.

If you want to be represented by a particular agent, but you are having a difficult time making a connection, here is something you can try. Job on your own, and ask the agent if he or she will handle the booking. Chances are the agent will be glad to represent you. It will be easily made money for the agent. The small percentage that you will lose will be well worth the connection you will have made.

If you are just beginning, do not sign long-term agreements with an agent you are unfamiliar with. If asked to sign, find out how many other models in your "category" are already signed. Your "category" includes other models that could be booked for the same job as you.

There will always be other signed models in your category. However, it is not in your best interest to be one of 50 others who could be submitted for the same job. If yours is the only agent sending models to a go-see, you have a much better chance of getting booked for the job if there are fewer models in your category. See if you can work out a trial period of three to six months. If you like the way you are being represented, sign a longer-term contract.

Before signing with an agent, make sure you understand everything in the contract. If you are not sure about something, show it to a lawyer.

Commercial models portray real people in all areas of advertising height and weight is rarely factors that determine whether you get the job or not. Being ethnic can be an added advantage thanks to the work of people like Tyson Beckford who was hired by Ralph Lauren.

Victoria's Secret used Tyra Banks there are many hosts of great ethnic models that, through handwork and persistence have adorned the cover of major magazines all over the world. You do not have to look like a supermodel to be successful as a model.

Commercial models come in all shapes, sizes and ages. Some commercial models are gorgeous men and women and some look like everyday people. The individual who has the greatest chance of being chosen to appear in an ad is the one who can believably look like a mom, dad, plumber, or a teacher.

The best part about commercial modeling is that you do not have to look "perfect" in order to be successful.

The job market for models is like a pyramid. At the base of the pyramid or (job market) are the standard fashion jobs. Like high fashion, commercial, and a large number of other jobs where they want someone "who looks like a model" (that's the tall, thin and beautiful people) As you move up this pyramid the amount of jobs get smaller such as plus size models and so on.

The Male Model

He should be tall generally about six feet to six two and as a rule you need to fit into a 40 regular to a 42 long jacket about 10% body fat and great clear skin is a plus. In today's market the classic good-looking guys are still in. But more and more offbeat, exotic, funky looking guys are getting booked, as an added plus, male model can work much longer, conceivably until there mid 40's.

The Female Model

She should be somewhat tall for high fashion modeling. Usually 5'8" to 5'7" although she may get away with being 5'6" She should be at 10% body fat hips no bigger than 35 inches the reason for this is fashion designers only make garment to be seen on runway and photo shoots so they make sample sizes to fit one body type. The age range is 12 to 25 but remembers there is exception and you may be that exception.

Now looking like a model is important. What do the advertisers want to see?

They want natural looking healthy looking guy and gals that can be turned into an exquisite image of beauty with saying that it is a good idea to stay away from tattoo and body piercing and also first impression count dress simple wear casual clothing avoid wearing logos. Wear clothing that fit right not to baggy think comfortable. Makeup should be clean or simple or none. Models hair should be healthy, shinny, clean and conditioned.

STEP TWO

Where do you fit in?

UNDERSTANDING YOUR BODY, HEALTH AND WELLNESS.

Let's talk about improving your body; everyone exercises for different reasons below is a list of reasons why you as a model should exercise. If you can find even one benefit from this list, you will have enough reason to begin an exercise program that will lead you to better health.

Regular exercise can . . .

- Help you lose weight, especially fat
- Improve your physical appearance
- Increase your level of muscular strength and endurance
- Maintain your resting metabolic rate, which will prevent weight gain
- Increase your stamina and ability to do continuous work
- Improve fitness levels, and your body's ability to use oxygen
- Provide protection against injury
- Improve your balance and coordination
- Increase bone mineral density to prevent osteoporosis and ostopenia.
- Lower resting heart rate and blood pressure
- Lower Body Mass Index (BMI) your fat to height ratio
- Enhance sexual desire and performance!
- Reduce heart disease risk and stroke

- Reduce the risk of developing certain types of cancer
- Increase insulin sensitivity, (prevents type 2 diabetes)
- Reduce your level of anxiety to help you manage stress
- Improve function of the immune system
- Improve your self-esteem and confidence You are working out four to five times a week and your are sore, but maybe you are not seeing the nice chest, legs, or arm that you would like to see. Here is some tip that might help you hit the goal.

Warm it up baby. Warm up your muscles with a five to ten minute low intensity cardio exercise. Whenever you raise the temperature of a muscle you decrease the risk of injury by making the muscle more pliable.

Where's the beef? The muscles in you body need protein to grow. The rule is you will need 1 gram of protein for every pound of your body's weight. Eating less than that can hold you back from hitting the goal. To help try some meal replacements such as protein bars and protein shakes.

Water please. Staying hydrated not only helps your muscles look great but it filters out after work out waste that can slow down protein metabolism and muscle growth. You'll need to drink 8-12 glasses of water a day. So drink-up!

Sweet dreams. Give yourself enough sleep to rebuild and time to release extra growth hormones. It is during sleep that muscles begin to rebuild themselves from the stresses of heavy lifting. You may need even more than eight hours of sleep.

Give me more reps. Using a weight that you can lift 8-12 reps per set will build muscle but if you are purely interested in toning or cutting up you need to use less weight and do 25 repetitions per set. This will cut you up and keep you lean.

THE GYM

If you are not a member of a local gym you should look into getting a membership it's worth the investment and remember your investing in you!

> You should perform strength training exercises 3-4 days/week with a minimal rest period of 48 hours between workouts. Start with a weight that you can lift for 8-12 repetitions. You should increase the weight once you can perform 12 repetitions with the weight that you are using. Strength training machines are recommended for beginners because they are generally safer than free weights. After you gain experience-using machines and your fitness level improves, you can incorporate free weights into your strength training routine.

How It Works:

Step 1

For training muscles of the upper body, use a repetition range of 8-12 repetitions. For the lower body, use a repetition range of 10-15. This means that you will be using a level of resistance (weight) that will bring you to momentary fatigue within the ranges listed above. Count and note the repetitions in this *first* set. If you can do more than 12 repetitions on this first set, the weights are probably too light. If less than 8, it's probably too heavy so adjust accordingly on your next workout. The same holds true for the lower body repetition ranges.—More than 15 "reps", and it's too light, less than 10 "reps", and it's a little too heavy. Again, adjust accordingly! Record the number of "reps" when the "sets" are completed.

Step 2

As soon as you have reached momentary muscle fatigue on the *first* set. Quickly reduce the resistance (weight) by approximately 25 to 30 percent. Immediately begin lifting the resistance and accomplish the maximum number of repetitions possible. Generally, this will be somewhere between 6 and 10 repetitions but responses on this second "quick set" vary widely.

Step 3

When Step 2 is completed, once again reduce the resistance (weight) by approximately 25 to 30 percent. Begin lifting as soon as possible with the reduced resistance (weight). You will find that even though it represents about 50 percent of the resistance with which you began, it is a challenging level of training that recruits maximum levels of muscle fibers with a level of intensity that elicits an optimal training effect. What's even more exciting is that you've accomplished the equivalent of three sets of training in approximately three or four minutes and can now move on to the next exercise or muscle group.

Modeling As Your Job

Step 4

Record the number of repetitions from Step I (Set #1) and adjust the resistance for your next workout based on the number of reps that you accomplished. *(See sample)* For example, for an upper body exercise, if you did 12 reps or more you should increase the weight slightly (approx. 1-2 percent) the next time you lift using that specific exercise (i.e.: adjust the weight <u>up</u>). If the number of reps is 8,9,10 or 11, the weight will remain the same the next time you lift. As presented earlier, if less than 8 reps are completed the weight is *too heavy* and needs to be reduced next time. Therefore, you will always be attempting to lift a little more resistance or another rep or two each time you train. These easy to establish goals will help keep you motivated.

Step 5

Move on to the next exercise or lift and repeat steps 1-4.

Just 30 minutes about 3 times per week and you've got the basic program that you need. And here's one more hint, train the larger muscles first (i.e.: chest and back) and work through the smaller muscles (i.e.: arms). It may take you a few workouts to establish all your start levels but once you do, your workout will be effective and much shorter in duration. And we could all use more time.

STEP TWO

Getting the job, getting the money let the games begin

YOUR MONEY AND JOBS JUST FOR SURVIVAL.

Credit-card debt

One of the most important things for the up and coming model is living a debt-free lifestyle. I've met many models that tell us they have credit card problems and when they open up their wallets you will see half a dozen credit cards. When ask why the answer is always the same "I got them for an emergency." Whatever!

If you have problems with credit card debt, you need to stop carrying them around. Why? So you cannot use them! You are going to learn a series of concrete ideas that will help you regain control of your credit card debt. Here's a hint: if you are spending more than 20% of your income paying off credit card debt, you have a problem. The best way I know of to pay off credit cards debt is by what I like to call debt termination. The debt termination program is about momentum. It is about getting all your cards, one after one "**done**." By **done** meaning you have paid off the balance and you have closed the account. "It's done." If you still feel you want one for an emergency (and I don't mean a fashion emergency!) or to build a credit record, that's fine. Here's how you do it. Take the current balance on each credit card statement and divide it by the minimum payment that the card company wants. And the result is your **done** number example, let's say the balance on your master card in $300.00 the company Wants $20.00 minimum payment. Dividing the total balance of $300.00 by the minimum payment of $20.00 gives you a done number of 10. Once you've figured out the done number of each account, rank them in reverse order.

In other words, the account with the lowest done number is the first one the one with the second-lowest number is second, and so on.

By doing this you know which cards can be paid off the fastest. Whatever you can afford to pay above your total required minimum payment for the month should be applied to the card with the lowest ranking **done**. Now when the first credit card has been paid off take the payment that you give to that first credit card and apply it to the second card.

And when the second is paid off you apply the money you paid for the first and second to the next bill till they're all **DONE**

STEP THREE

SO YOU WANT TO BE IN PICTURES

STEP THREE

So you want to be in pictures

CHANGING THE WAY YOU THINK.

<u>Here are six keys that I believe are the keys to having the right mindset</u>

1) <u>You need to have a passion for modeling</u>.

You have to think about modeling all the time, dream about it, talk about it, read books, magazines, and see fashion shows. It must consume you because whatever you focus on will grow. If you focus on problems like bills, your relationship, family issues, the car, your job or whatever it may be, it will grow. You will be amazed at how much you focus on seems to grow. You need to stay focused on your career.

2) <u>Believe in what you are doing</u>.

Belief is a powerful thing you can move mountains and if you can dream it you can do it. There is nothing you cannot do. Having said that, if you believe you cannot, you're right. Be very careful of what you tell yourself because you will start to believe it. Things like I am not good looking or that you are fat, ugly, to short or too tall. If it's not positive do not say it to yourself, and if someone says it to you do not believe it. Think to you, that is there belief and that's ok but it is not mine. Do not take ownership of that believe.

3) <u>Have a game plan.</u>

If you do not have a game plan it is like a sailboat with no sail. No direction it is just sitting there wherever the current takes it. This is no way to go through life. You the model must have a game plan. Start with what it is that you want and set the goal. You will need to see where you want to be one year. Then you'll need to break it down into quarters, So that you're focusing on 90-day increments. For example, "I want to lose 40 pounds" So 40 pounds divided into 4 quarters are 10 pounds per quarter divided that by 3 months in a quarter. That is 3 pounds a month you see how much easier that is when are taking baby steps and inch-by-inch it's a synch!

4) <u>Your values; you must be clear and balanced.</u>

Have you ever met someone who loves to tan but hates the fact that they're getting older?

Or you want to be rich, but love to go shopping, hangout, and spend lot of money? You say one thing but your actions say another. This is called inner civil war. What you say and what you do must be balance or you're not going to be successful.

You have to stop the war.

5) <u>Affirmation, what you tell yourself.</u>

I guess the best way to describe affirmations is; to repeat something that you want to manifest over and over till you believe it, can be done so that when you believe it you do not have fear to stop you.

There are 7 guild lines

    A) It must start with "I am."
    B) It must be stated positively.
    C) It must be in the present state.
    D) It needs to be brief.
    E) It must be clear with an "ing" word in it.
    F) It should have a feeling word in it.
    G) It should be an affirmation about you.

Now you have to say your affirmation 2 times a day. As soon as you get up in the morning and before you go to bed at night. Maybe write them down on a 3 x 5 card.

Example **"I am happily go<u>ing</u> on go and see's 5 times a week every week in a way that is moving me closer to becoming a super model"**

6) <u>Who you surround yourself with</u>.

You the model must surround yourself with positive people. Friends, family, and co-workers that support and believe in what you're doing and won't put you down. People that are moving in the same direction, maybe other models, agents, booker's people who are also focused like you on the business. This way, you will always stay focused. Because this business is hard enough and you don't need someone to bring you down.

STEP THREE

So you want to be in pictures

TIME MANAGEMENT THE ABILITY TO MANAGE YOURSELF.

You know when it comes to your photo and managing your time. I would say that the best piece of advice that I can give you is that its not something that need to be rushed you can take your time as long as you are aware and in the process of getting the photos done. The most important lesson here is you need to be comfortable in front of a camera. If you are stressing or uncomfortable it will show in the photograph.

Maybe you should have your picture taken once a week or every other week at worst once a month. I would venture to say that once a month is safe.

Just to get yourself comfortable in front of the camera.

My thinking here is it's so early in the game that although you need to start getting photos taken you has time. But make sure your managing yourself. Here a cool idea that you can have fun with. Look though magazines or Google Models for hire and look at how the pictures or taken so that you can have a better idea of what looks professional and doesn't.

And just remember this is to market you so take your time learn. There is no room for shyness. Always remember never sign a release to a photographer unless he is paying you for the photo and even then I would think it over long and hard. You never know then you least expect it the photos you took 20 years ago when you was up and coming pop up to haunt you.

Just don't dismiss this area of your training and development.

By the time you land an agent you should have tons of pictures to choose from. By the way this process will never end, you see you can't market yourself with photo of then you were ten years younger, the photo must be fresh and current. So you might as well get use to the idea of getting photograph. Here is another idea you should have famed photos of yourself all over you apartment or room for you to see all day everyday your friend and family will think you have gone nuts or your just full of yourself. Understanding how you look is what you're doing so that you can better sell yourself. Now lets move on to the business.

STEP THREE

So you want to be in pictures

GETTING DOWN TO THE FUNDAMENTALS OF THE BUSINESS, I MEAN MODELING BUSINESS.

First you must learn how to pose and move naturally but effectively, you must become one, with the photographer and you must become a master at taking directions the best way to become a master at taking direction is working with as many different photographers as you can. One way is by getting test shoots. Test shoots are for experience only and they will not land you a job test shoots will help you get comfortable in the environment of a photo studio. Before you begin you will want to get to know the vision or image the photographer is trying to convey. Test shoots should not be too costly; no more than $100.00 per roll do not spend any money on test photos.

Get a good nights sleep and stay healthy if you are tired it will show on your face and in your attitude so do not party the night before the shoot. Arrive on time better yet get to the shoot 15 minutes before your to arrive it is a part of being a professional. Now you will need to review with the photographer to see how to proceed with the shoot what is the game plan?

Communication is the key you need to follow the verbal instructions of the photographer and provide feedback. As you the model and photographer work together more, the process becomes easier also you will need to understand that there may come a time during the shoot when it is quicker and easier for the photographer to physically move you. Your arms head and legs. If you are uncomfortable with this state it up front. Now how do you find a photographer?

What are some strategies for tracking down photographers for free test shoots? One-way might be to check a photographer's web site just go online and do a search. Start off with your town.

Find ones in your area and see if any of them do model photography. You can also try calling around or visiting photographer studios. But that will take more work. The yellow pages might be helpful in your pursuit. You will need to shop around and check photographers' portfolios to find the one that is doing good and quality work. Again, checking photographers' web sites can help with this. At the beginning of your modeling career, your portfolio should include no more than 3-5 pictures.

The photo that you want are three basic types; face, body and personality

The face: to see how you look with a range of expressions.

The body: When posing makes sure your body is full of energy and is working do not look limp.

The personality: will give you an idea of who you can become when the camera is pointed at you.

The photographer will show you something called a contact sheet, which is a large sheet of photographic paper that has mini pictures that were shot. Study which photos you like the best, and maybe ask the photographer which ones are the best you may want some prints although not necessary.

STEP THREE

So you want to be in pictures

UNDERSTANDING YOUR BODY, HEALTH AND WELLNESS.

I would like for you to watch a documentary on HuLu witch is a website offering ad-supported streaming of videos, TV shows and documentaries. I found this documentary but if you find that it is no longer offered then simply Google It. The name of the documentary is Fat sick and nearly dead which follows Joe Cross for 60 days across America as he juice fast to regain his health. Following his fast he adopts a plant-based diet and loses 100 pounds and stops all medication and so I'm not saying this is something you should do. What I am giving you are options, so check it out.

STEP THREE

So you want to be in pictures

YOUR MONEY AND JOBS JUST FOR SURVIVAL.

In step three on the topic of your money I want to spend some time talking to you about your financial knowledge. So that you know what to do when the cash starts to flow and you are not mislead by other.

Now remember every goal has a processes and when it comes to your money it's the same, the reason why so many actor struggle with finances is because they don't want to be bothered with the processes of learning about money, some don't even know how to balance a checkbook.

The reason so many people don't become working actor is they fail to focus on the process and with money the same applies learn the processes and apply it.

Here is an example of what I'm talking about, have you ever heard of a lottery winner losing all of his/her money after a few years of winning the money? It is because he/she never learned the processes of making money; the money was just handed to them. It's all too common.

One of the biggest problem up and coming actor have is learn to control is their need for instant gratification.

They have to have the latest toys that come to market and the hottest fashion by the best and hottest designers paying thousands for it.

Not realizing that if they just focus on the process and become successful, most designers will loan them the outfit and or jewelry for free, and in a lot of cases let them keep there latest design as long as they promise the say the designers name in public. When you look at most award shows and you see the beautiful gown and the beautiful jewelry why do you think they are always asked? "You look amazing who are you wearing?"

But if you still think this is going to be really heard to do then focus on landing a job in a retail store in your local mall most are open late this way you can go out on audition during the day and work at night, so that not only are you making part time cash but you are getting an employee discount to shop. So listen to the voice of reason use that money for your pictures instead.

Now I'm going to give you some homework. My favorite financial guru is Robert Kiyosaki he has a book called increase your finical IQ I'm asking you to read it, notice I didn't say buy it, I say read it. It wills if you apply its principles change your life. And again I'm in no way affiliated with any of his books or companies. I am just sharing with you what I have learned.

I want to share a story with you, a few years back while living in New York City I made a friend who moved to the city with the dream of breaking into the Broadway musical since. And the first thing he did when he got to the city was land a job with a photographer as his assistant. One day while having lunch I asked him why of all the jobs in the city did he get a job as an assistant to a photographer?

And the answer he gives me I found to be brilliant. He told me that while growing up in the Midwest, as a kid he was very shy and hated having his picture taken, he always felt unattractive, and by working with a photographer he would overcome his shyness by leaning what a photographer looks for in his subjects, plus he continued to say "I get all my pictures taken for free while getting paid to learn the business. What if you did the same, maybe as an intern? The city is filled with up and coming photographers freshly out of school looking to make a name for themselves and can't afford to pay an assistance and are willing to work with interns till they make it big. So you get free photographs and the photographer gets free help. *What a beautiful barter.*

STEP FOUR

CHANGING THAT SILLY THINKING

STEP FOUR

Changing that silly thinking

CHANGING THE WAY YOU THINK.

Here's something for you to think about. Have you ever told someone or even warned someone about a situation that you knew they were about to get into that maybe was a bad situation for them.

Or maybe you've been there before and you just want to warn them about it and they just won't listen to what you have to say? And a few months later your friends or this person is in trouble, and you just want to scream "I told you so you never listen!"

Do you know why this is?

It's simple really, as your warning the person or friend they are thinking to themselves "That's not going to happen to me because I'm smarter than you are"

So they don't even hear what you are saying, at all, to the point that when you do say "I told you so" they don't even remember you warning them at all. ***Don't be that person***!

Ok moving on, I want to share something with you that have had a profound impacted in my life and maybe if I share it with you, it can do the same for you.

One day while watching the Oprah Winfrey show (don't judge me!) a segment on the power of gratitude was on, and how Oprah and her guests used gratitude in their lives to changes that happens to them. After just a few minutes I was hooked, when the show was over I started looking into this and once again I called on my friend Google.

There were hundreds of books and articles on the subject. Let me give you short synopsis of what I have read and learned. But if you have the time please look into the topic for yourself you never know I may be nuts.

The idea is, and I am so sold on this idea, that gratitude is the greatest amplifier. It literally amplifies, doubling or even gives you more of all the things that you are thankful for. You can turnaround anything in your life through the use of gratitude and I mean anything, from your fiancés, to broken relationship even your health.

Why do you think Jesus always said thank you before he performed every miracles? Ever time you are thankful you are giving love and whatever you give you will receive. It doesn't matter if you're giving thanks to a person or money no matter how small the amount, a car, a parking spot, the light changing or a vacation. You are giving love for those things and you will receive more of these things.

More health, more money and more amazing things will come into your life then you learn to be grateful. If the only pray you ever say in you life is thank you that is enough. Gratitude is simple it start with thank you. But make sure you're feeling grateful with all your heart the more you say thank you the more real and genuine it will become and the more love you will begin to feel.

Here is how you are going to start using gratitude to change your life. I got this idea from Oprah, ever night before she falls asleep she writes down all the things she was grateful for that happened to her during the day.

I can't do it this way, what I do is every morning before I get out of bed I have a pad that I call my gratitude pad where I write all the amazing things that happened to me the day before. There are three ways to use the power of gratitude.

First be grateful for everything you have received in you life, that's being grateful for the passed.

The second is to be grateful for everything your receiving in your life, that's being grateful for the present.

Third is being grateful for all the things you want in your life as if you have already received it, in your life. That's being grateful for the future.

When you're grateful for what you have received and what you are continuing to receive it multiplies those things. At the same time gratitude brings you the things your want so always be grateful for the thing you want in your life as if you have received them already. So are you sold on the idea?

Get yourself a small pad and pen put it by your nightstand and writes down what your grateful for daily.

Give it a shot what do you have to lose, its working for me.

STEP FOUR

United we stand divided we fall!

TIME MANAGEMENT THE ABILITY TO MANAGE YOURSELF.

Now before we go gun hole trying to get into one of the unions you are going to need to get some experience under your belt. So the focus still is and will continue to be mastering your craft that is the most important lesion. For now I want you to know everything there is to know about all the different unions.

Set aside time to research the unions know everything there is to know about the different union. When was the union started? Why was the union started and by whom? What is the union's focus and or mission statement? Down to which famous celebrities are in which union. Let's not forget what are all the benefits each union offers its members. You should know the in and out of all the major unions. So set aside the time to make this happen. All of this is going to require some time and the great thing here is you don't need to get it all done at once. Just set aside an hour or so weekly, just to research one union at the time. Simply manager your time carefully and you can get it all done. By the time your ready to join one of the great unions you will know everything there is to know about the union your ultimately decide to join.

One thing you should consider doing as you move through this journey and meet people in business is that in conversation always asks what union they are a part of and why did they choose that particular union. You'll be amazed on the wealth of information you will get just by asking.

Always remember in this business it's not what you know it's whom you know so let's make lots of friends. And when its time to get into one of the union you may have to call upon one of your new friends to help open a few doors. Now in the in the next step I'll be going over in more detail the business side of the unions however this doesn't mean you don't have to set aside the time to do the research yourself.

<u>Your ability to manager yourself will determine how successful you ultimately become.</u>

STEP FOUR

United we stand divided we fall!

GETTING DOWN TO THE FUNDAMENTALS OF THE BUSINESS, I MEAN SHOW MODELING BUSINESS.

As your quest begins, you need to be very careful unfortunately in today's world, for every five models there is a scam out there. You must be on guard and if it sounds too good to be true it is. Below is a list of how to spot scams. There is no way to get them all every day someone is thinking of a way to get your money. So be on your toes.

1. Photographers and so called talent scouts prey on young unsuspecting models offering to help them get an agent they start by suggesting a lot of professional pictures, composites and portfolios, these people are probably just trying to make money off of the photo session if anyone tells you that you need to spend all a lot of money in order to break into the business they're scamming you grab your bags and run.

2. Two of the most common things offered by modeling scam artists are modeling photos of a quality or quantity, which new and aspiring models do not need, and training which a model does not need, or if it is needed, the reputable agency provides it free. The credibility of a modeling agency and the possibility of a modeling photography scam can be evaluated to some extent based on whether only one photographer is required or recommended. Reputable agencies should give a list of top photographers, but they will not require one photographer.

3. Guaranteed work
4. Conflict of interest
5. Upfront fees
6. High prices
7. High sales pressure
8. Manipulation to use specific photographer
9. No tear sheets
10. Agency makes profit from photography
11. No agency license
12. Address is only a PO Box number, not a street address
13. Nothing in writing the Overall impression of the company is really most interested in making/taking money
14. Business plan designed for fast, easy money
15. The "free open call" or "free audition" is nothing more than a contrived meeting for a sales pitch
16. It would be difficult to hold the company accountable if the model signed a contract because the agency is in another state
17. Business partnerships which create conflict of interest (e.g. schools with agency; schools)
18. Most models make less money than they pay for photos
19. Late payments for completed work
20. Leaders have history of fraud
21. Published news reports allege fraud, greed, corruption
22. The words "scam" or "fraud" are often used in online discussions of the company
23. Local media issued warnings and consumer alerts
24. Oral representations different from written representations
25. Emphasis of marketing to aspiring models is the future potential not the past;
26. No client list

27. Pricing not on website
28. Hidden fees
29. Extra expenses not communicated
30. Not up front about basic important issue(s)
31. Training not free
32. Online portfolio not free
33. Website address of "professional photographer" not provided
34. Company has its own photographer or own photo studio
35. Pictures taken by photographer do not look professional
36. High fees for web portfolio
37. Professional photos for infants
38. Professional photos for kids under four years old
39. Leaders previously prosecuted by the Federal Trade Commission
40. State consumer protection agency issued warnings and consumer alerts

STEP FOUR

United we stand divided we fall!

UNDERSTANDING YOUR BODY, HEALTH AND WELLNESS.

STEPS TO ATTAINING A PERFECT TEN BODY IMAGE

- Don't skip breakfast
- Eat fruits and veggies
- Drink plenty of water
- Limit sugar and fat intake
- Don't crash diet
- Don't deprive yourself of occasional treats
- Don't eat during the RED ZONE (between 9 PM and 6 AM)
- Join an aerobics class
- Power walking
- Tai Chi

It may seem like a lot to do. Remember, this is you job this is how you put food on the table and pay the bills.

Controlling stress

Stress affects your emotional well being how you feel about you and your health so it needs to be addressed. I like to think of stress as a dark cloud over one's head. It doesn't let you think right everything is overwhelming you feel like your world is coming to an end. Happy and stress-free living will help you remain focus and productive. One of the best ways to reduce stress is to exercise. Exercise metabolizes stress hormones in your blood and increases levels of your bodies built in ant anxiety hormones, making you feel calmer.

Simple exercises like walking regularly can increase the level of beta-endorphins in the brain, decrease anxiety and tension, and elevate your mood. Combined programs like yoga that include both body stretching and mind relaxation can be especially effective in easing emotional and physical tensions.

One thing that many models find stressful is the sense that they do not have any control over a given situation, especially when they have many demands on their time. If this happens to you try to think about the situation you find stressful from a different perspective. Is it really that bad? Is there another way of looking at the problem? If you cannot avoid a stress-producing situation, approach it in a calculated way, taking step to avoid the stress. Develop coping skills learn to take a time-out when you start to feel your anxiety rise. Here's a big one-watch lots of comedy movies in your free time. Laughter is the best ways to keep stress it check many studies show that laughter is the best way to deal with stress and its fun too.

We may not ever fit into society's measure of a perfect 10 body but a perfect 10 body image is definitely attainable. Below I have outlined a few simple steps.

STEP FOUR

United we stand divided we fall!

YOUR MONEY AND JOBS JUST FOR SURVIVAL.

The money game

As I said before modeling is a business and understanding money is an important aspect of any business. How you handle your money then is vary important. If you do not, you will be out of business before your start. The number one reason why up and coming models struggle is because they have no idea how to handle there money their live beyond their means and they spend more than they make. One way of handling your funds is what is called the rule of 25%.

- A) 25% of your income should go to savings
- B) 25% of your income should go to you; party money, shopping and hanging out with friends
- C) 25% to rent
- D) 25% to bills

Lets break it down. Lets assume for this example your monthly income is $1000.00

- A) $250.00 goes to saving
- B) $250.00 goes to you
- C) $250.00 goes to rent
- D) $250.00 goes to bills

Now you may be thinking my rent is much more than that well you are living be on your means. You can increase your income or decrease your expenses, but something has to give. And taking from the savings to help pay the rent is not a solution.

Your saving is the single most important aspect, like all business, there are dry times when nothing's going in its slow, and no work is coming in. Then how are you going to pay the bills that when you're saving become, the backup. It may not seem like much but if you took $250.00 times six months that is $1500.00 and you're still in business. It's as simple as that. But it's going to take focus.

STEP FIVE

HAVE YOUR PEOPLE, CALL MY PEOPLE, THE AGENT

STEP FIVE

Have your people, call my people, the agent

CHANGING THE WAY YOU THINK.

When it comes to the agent in this stage of the game or the process, you must be proactive. Although the agent works for you, you don't work for the agent.

The agent gets paid when you get paid, with that being said you must become proactive making sure you're in the back of the mind of the agent at all times.

Remember the agent gets paid when you get paid, however your not the agents only client, this agent he/she may have up to one hundred active clients and some might be already established models or even superstars.

So when your agents gets a call looking for a specific type, that type might be your type, but your agent may have several clients that fit that type as well, that he/she is working with, and there is a saying that says, "The squeaky wheel gets the oil" You need to be that squeaky wheel.

That is why you must call the agent on an ongoing basis weekly maybe even two or three times a week. You must become the agents best friend and always be in contact with the agent, simply put the agent has a lot on his or her mind remember this is a business and he/she is trying to make a living.

Now's its time to work harder than ever.

Did you know that 80% of all the models that are in an agency never get booked in today's market only 20% gets booked.

Why you ask? Because the 20% know that it is a partnership between the booker and the model.

The model calls his or her booker 3-4-5 time a day. The working model goes out and networks with clients, advertisers, and other agencies, meets new photographers that could be looking for a new face to shoot. You the new kid on the block must do the same. I've have met so many talented models who get booked once a month and talk about how they're on the way to being a supermodel.

Their dreaming, not that there's anything wrong with dreaming, but at this stage of the game its time to get to work.

You must continue to do the things that got you this far and a little more. Focus on work! Work hard, play hard win, win, win! Also it is important to know the kind of behavior that is acceptable for a models being rude or throwing tantrums every time something did not go your way is not acceptable.

Always treat people the way you would like to be treated or you will not stay in business very long.

Look the fact of the matter is the model who is more established and well know, if the agent has one of those in his/her active client list he will pull that model out first because he/she knows the client will want

Modeling As Your Job

that model and the agent will get paid, if your less recognized then you become that last resource to that agent to try and land the deal.

This is why we are talking about becoming proactive and following up with the agent. The name of the game is follow-up. And always make sure that your agent or booker is working with you, always trying and making an effort the find you work.

Make sure your accessible at all times to the agent so that he/she can send you on go and see even on weekends or traveling on vacation, make sure you can be reached.

You must put yourself in a position that when your agent or bookers phone rings and they ask for a type you're the first person that pops in that persons head. That has to be your mindset in the beginning sage of your modeling career. You can't party and hangout and have a good time, if your going to be a working model.

So I need you change the way your thinking and understand this is a partnership you have with your agent and together you will find work Bare in mind he/she has a financial interest in you and your career at the same time you must take ownership of this entire process.

STEP FIVE

Have your people, call my people, the agent

TIME MANAGEMENT THE ABILITY TO MANAGE YOURSELF.

Now in this step of time management we are going to collapse time. What I need you to do is watch a documentary and I promise you this will be the best time you have ever spend watching a movie. This documentary will open you eyes to the real world of high fashion.

Remember high fashion modeling is not the only modeling that is out there and not the only modeling this book is focused on, there is commercial modeling, Sport Modeling and Part Modeling such as Hand Modeling and Leg Models anyway you get my point. As of the writing of the book on HuLu witch is a website offering ad-supported streaming of videos, TV shows and documentaries. I found this documentary but if you find that it is no longer offered then simply Google It. The name of the documentary is Picture Me: A Models Diary it's a look at the inner world of Modeling. I Google it to see what some of the critic were saying about it and this is what I found.

Film Review: Picture Me: A Model's Diary

This absorbing, highly personal documentary gives a stripped-down, inside look at a glamorous business, which can often be anything but.

Sept 17, 2010

—By David Noh

Picture Me: A Model's Diary focuses on the world of fashion models, specifically that of Sara Ziff, who co-directed and co-produced the film. A 23-year-old blonde with the kind of ideal blank-canvas mannequin face that can be alternately rather ordinary or made up to look smolderingly glamorous, she is, unbelievably, already considered old for a career known for throwing 14-year-olds on the runway. The film actually takes her from the age of 18 and reveals her gradual disillusionment with the catwalk.

It's a particularly clear-eyed look at this most outwardly alluring of worlds, touching on many of the industry's dirty little not-so-secrets, like the dangerous emphasis on skinniness which make even wraithlike girls like Ziff feel fat in comparison to those adolescents who are constantly coming up for coveted jobs. Other models—many of whom lie about their ages when auditioning for jobs although none is over 24—weigh in with their opinions and reminiscences of the dehumanizing treatment they've encountered, being openly discussed in terms of their (non-existent) body fat as if they were deaf slabs of meat. The compromising positions these heartbreakingly young girls are sometimes thrown into, alone and lacking any parental guidance in foreign cities, are also addressed, with a model recalling how she had to roughly manipulate a well-known photographer's penis in order to book a job. "I didn't feel good about it afterwards," she says, "or when I told my boyfriend about it." Ziff's parents are interviewed, a university professor and a lawyer, who express astonishment that their child is already earning more money than they are, and is also the first person in their families not to bother with a proper education. Her boyfriend also appears, totally gob smacked by a $112,000 paycheck she receives. The downside of such financial power is revealed when Ziff complains about always having to pay for him, while being cognizant of the fact that "unless you date some 40 or 50-year-old banker, no one your age will be earning as much as you." However inflated models' salaries seem to be, there's no doubt that they work hard for it, especially during fashion season when they must jet from Milan to New York to Paris in a matter of days, rushing from show to show, sans proper sleep or nourishment. An exhausted Ziff has something of a meltdown, her face covered in stress-related pimples, as she tearfully recounts how photographers pushed their way backstage and shot her in the nude as she changed, numb to her pleas for them to stop. For this scene alone, any serious-minded parent, worried over a willful child's fantasy of pursuing a modeling career, would do well to show them this film. Now watch it and lets move on.

STEP FIVE

Have your people, call my people, the agent

GETTING DOWN TO THE FUNDAMENTALS OF THE BUSINESS, I MEAN MODELING BUSINESS.

Test shoots for your professional portfolio are also referred to as test shoots for your book. The reason you do them is have photo to put in your portfolio. Your portfolio is then shown to potential clients and agencies give the client an idea of how well you photograph. The model is responsible for paying for the test shoot, but in most cases if you have landed an agency before the photo session the agency will pay for it in advance.

They will deduct the money from the first job usually $500.00 plus the cost of film processing.

Depending on the stage of your modeling career, photos for your portfolio, composite cards, the agency book and the agency head sheet come from two major sources:

They are taken at a test shoot for your portfolio, or they are tear sheets (pages torn from a magazine, newspaper, or other periodical) from an advertisement or editorial photo shoot you've appeared in. If a model is just starting out and hasn't worked yet, he or she would use the photos from the test shot for the portfolio. But once a model starts working, their test shots are gradually replaced by examples of their professional work or tear sheets. Your agency will get tear sheets for all the work you do.

PJ Medina

Often, the magazine or catalog company will send those copies, or the agency may subscribe to the publication them.

Your portfolio is a leather or vinyl bound album about 12"x15" models carry their portfolio to every go and see once you start working, your agency will supply you with tear sheets. Always remember your portfolio represents who you are, if it is sloppy or dirty it reflects badly on you. Your Portfolio should always be neat, clean and organized.

At every photo session you will need to sign a model release form. When a photo is taken and your image is captured, you have certain rights with regards to that photo.

These generally revolve around personal privacy and commercial exploitation rights. The model release is a legal form that releases or transfers those rights to someone else. What it comes down to is the photographer, ad agency or final client cannot use your pictures unless you give them permission, and if you do not give your permission you do not work. Part of being a model, like being an actor, is to give up some of your privacy. You become a public figure and you expect to be compensated for this loss of privacy.

Below you'll see a sample of a photo release form.

<u>MODEL RELEASE</u>

I, _____
_____ do hereby give to _____(the Photographer), his or her assigns, licensees, successors in interest, legal representatives, and heirs the irrevocable right to use my name (or any fictional name),

picture, portrait, or photograph in all forms and in all media and in all manners, without any restriction as to changes or alterations (including but not limited to composite or distorted representations or derivative works made in any medium) for advertising, trade, promotion, exhibition, or any other lawful purposes, and I waive any right to inspect or approve the photograph(s) or finished version(s) incorporating the photograph(s), including written copy that may be created and appear in connection therewith.

I hereby release and agree to hold harmless the Photographer, his or her assigns, licensees, successors in interest, legal representatives and heirs from any liability by virtue of any blurring, distortion, alteration, optical illusion, or use in composite form whether intentional or otherwise, that may occur or be produced in the taking of the photographs, or in any processing tending toward the completion of the finished product, unless it can be shown that they and the publication thereof were maliciously caused, produced, and published solely for the purpose of subjecting me to conspicuous ridicule, scandal, reproach, scorn, and indignity. I agree that the Photographer owns the copyright in these photographs and I hereby waive any claims I may have based on any usage of the photographs or works derived there from, including but not limited to claims for either invasion of privacy or libel. I am of full age and competent to sign this release. I agree that this release shall be binding on legal representatives, my heirs, assigns, and me.

I have read this release and am fully familiar with its contents.

Model: _____   Signed: _____
Address: _____

PJ Medina

Date: _____, 19 _____

Consent (if applicable)

I am the parent or guardian of the minor named above and have the legal authority to execute the above release. I approve the foregoing and waive any rights in the premises.

Witness: _____   Signed: _____

COMP CARDS OR COMPOSITE CARDS

Comp card are your business cards, just like any other business you the model must have comp card that are 8 ½" x 6" cards. It should features several different shots of you. It is given to all clients, so they can get an idea of your look.

Don't bent, crumple or dirty your cards they should always look professional and neat about 100 to 200 comp card are printed at a time The ultimate success of a comp card comes down to the quality of the photographs. The quality of the photographs comes from the quality and talent of the model and the professionalism and creativity of the photographer and his team. To have an effective comp card you need to start with an excellent set of photographs. Most important is an eye-catching, grab-your-attention-from-across-the-office headshot for the front of the card.

You can have great photos and a poorly produced comp card and still come out with something useful. Bad photos and bad production will indicate you are not a professional. Of course top photos; innovative design and top comp card production will announce you as a top-tier professional model. Besides a great head-shot, the comp card will have other photos that show your experience, your versatility, range, and the type of work you are seeking.

For best results all of the photos should be of the highest quality that you can obtain.

When a model lands an agent, the agency pays for the comp card then deducts the cost from the model's pay they usually the cost is anywhere from $100. To $300, Depending on how many card you order they should be update about once a year.

STEP FIVE

Have your people, call my people, the agent

UNDERSTANDING YOUR BODY, HEALTH AND WELLNESS.

Here my warning!

I would like to make this very clear. Nothing well make you more sick then money problems so As you begin your quest of becoming a model there may come a time where you may ask yourself "where am I ever going to get the money to even start". Well that is why you got this book!

The problem is not how much you make. It is how much you spend! There is a game plan for the next seven months; you are going to tap into what I call the <u>you</u> money fund.

This is the money that I mentioned was going to be used for fun, shopping and hanging out. In that past example we used $250.00. You're going to put half of that away and only spend $125.00 per month. I know what you are thinking, "what can I do with so little." I did not say it was going to be easy. It is going to be worth it. You are going to save $125.00 for seven months. In the meantime you are focusing on completing this book and implementing the things you have learned.

Let do the math $125.00 x 7 = $875.00

Not bad you just started your own business with $875.00 how many people do you know that can say that. It may not sound like all the money in the world but it is a start. You can join a gym, start that new diet, or get some test shoots.

STEP FIVE

So you want to be in pictures

YOUR MONEY AND JOBS JUST FOR SURVIVAL.

Show me the money

A go and see is a job interview for a modeling job. Although you the model may have your book filled with great shoots, clients want to know what you are like in person also sometimes models photograph different from how they look like due to makeup, lighting and touchup. Your booker will set up your go and see a week or a day in advance believe me go/sees can be very hard and depressing experiences. Always make sure you have with you your appointment book, portfolio, comp cards, a cell phone and high heels if you're doing runway. Always repeat some positive affirmations while you wait and don't get caught up in client's negative comments.

Models are paid through a voucher system usually the voucher comes in a book form that contains about 20 vouchers. You the model will carry these vouchers to every job there it is signed by the client confirming that you worked. You then submit the signed copy to the agency's accounting department, which then bills the client and pays you. Do not ever make the mistake of not getting your voucher signed if any problem comes up, that piece of paper is concrete documentation of the time you worked and the amount you are owed.

It is estimated that $100,000 a year is the standard earning of the average working model. Remembers. Because modeling is so lucrative trying to get hired for a job is a difficult thing. One thing you do not want to do is not pay your tax's because no tax's are withheld from your pay a model has to pay his/her own tax's on a quarterly basis.

STEP SIX

BOOKING WHOM?

STEP SIX

Booking Whom?

CHANGING THE WAY YOU THINK.

Never argue with a fool, from a distance people can't tell who is who.

Now look here, I know I've touched on this earlier in this book but please trust and believe me when I tell you this is detrimental to your career. So let me break it down for you my friend, people will not always be nice to you and say thing that are rude or hurtful just kill them with kindness.

Now fewer things are more frustrating then the wait to hear if you have been casted. With great luck, the director, producer, or your agent will telephone you within 24 hours. But several days may go by before you hear anything, and it is all too easy to drive yourself crazy wondering. Remember your job is to give a great audition.

All you can do is all you can do.

Put yourself in the director's shoes. If you were casting a show, would you make up your mind in a couple of hours about who to cast in a dozen roles?

Of course not, you might even need to think about it for a couple of days and the larger the cast the more thought it might take. What's more the difficulties that the director faces in making a decision overlap.

While the female lead may be a single obvious choice, for example, the male lead could have two or three contenders. Deciding between them isn't often just a matter of concluding which would be the best for the lead role.

You just make sure your voice mail and e-mail address is working and that you can check them from your mobile phone. It's important to be as accessible as possible to casting agents and directors. Lets move on.

STEP SIX

Booking Whom?

TIME MANAGEMENT THE ABILITY TO MANAGE YOURSELF.

The compounding effects of your efforts

Lets assume that till this point you have followed all the steps but nothing or very little works in coming your way. You have to give your efforts time to compound. What does this mean? Simply put in the beginning all the work of running around, the rejections, and the entire no's.

You are putting in so much effort and getting very little or no results but with time you are going to put very little effort and get a lot of result. Were you are running around all day from photo shoot to photo shoot and the money is pouring in! But in the beginning you have to work your tail off and believe in yourself.

Let me tell you a story of a model we met who at the time was starting his career as a model and for two year could not find an agent that liked his look. Being skinny, tall, and black with a big afro. Till one day while visiting this mother down south he got a call that changed everything. A designer was interested in using his look for a new fall runway show. So he did the show and his cell phone hasn't stopped ring. And now today look in any magazine and you'll find tons of tall, skinny, black men with afros in its pages. So be very careful of starting to think that maybe modeling is not for you. You will start to think that you are not cut out to be a model or that you should throw in the towel. We call this stinky thinking. Remember to control what you tell yourself. You can not allow the process to stress you out you the model can not control if an agent doesn't like you or think badly of your look or you are not the one for a particular fashion spread. All you can control is you! Your focus, your vision, putting yourself out there every day following and the step you have learned here, and controlling your time and being productive.

STEP SIX

Booking Whom?

GETTING DOWN TO THE FUNDAMENTALS OF THE BUSINESS, I MEAN THE MODELING BUSINESS.

Representation TIME

You need to understand that there are different agencies for different looks. Fashion models and commercial models are two different markets, styles, and requirements per agency. Both types of careers require confidence, personality and competence. Its time to send out your comp cards. Representation is the biggest step.

Below is a listing of modeling agencies:

ACME
875 6th Ave Suite 2108
NY, NY 10001
Phone: 212-328-0388

ABRAMS ARTISTS AGENCY
275 Seventh Ave. #26th Floor
NY, NY 10001
Phone: 646-486-4600
http://www.abramsartists.com
vincent.devito@abramsart.com

A PLUS MODELS LTD
18 West 21st St.
NEW YORK, NY 10011
Phone: (212) 633-1990

BELLA AGENCY
270 Lafayette Street # 802
NY, NY 10012
Phone: 212-965-9200
http://www.bellaagency.com
rvolant@bellaagency.com

BOSS MODELS INC
1 GANSEVOORT ST
NEW YORK, NY 10014
Phone: (212) 242-2444
Web Site: http://www.bossmodels.com/

CLICK MODEL MANAGEMENT
129 west 27th St.,
NEW YORK, NY 10001
3RD FLOOR
NEW YORK, N.Y. 10011
212.638.3330
Web Site: www.karinmodels.com

M MODEL MANAGEMENT, INC
352 SEVENTH AVE, 4TH FL.
NEW YORK, NY 10001
Phone: (212) 631-7551

Represents Men/Women for Fashion and Commercial Print. Mail in Comps.

METROPOLITAN MODEL MANAGEMENT
5 W UNION SQ # 5
NEW YORK, NY 10003
Phone: (212) 989-0100
Fax: (212) 989-6911

NEXT MANAGEMENT CO
23 WATTS ST # 5
NEW YORK, NY 10013
Phone: (212) 925-2225
Fax: (212) 925-5931

NEW YORK MODEL MANAGEMENT
149 WOOSTER ST.
7TH FLOOR
NEW YORK, N.Y. 10012
(212) 539-1700
(212) 539-1775
Web Site: www.newyorkmodels.com

OHM MODEL MANAGEMENT
1133 BROADWAY #910
NEW YORK, N.Y. 10010
(212) 989 6395
Web Site: www.ohmmodels.com

PAULINE'S MODEL MANAGEMENT
379 W BROADWAY
NEW YORK, NY 10012
Phone: (212) 941-6000
Fax: (212) 274-0434

Q NEW YORK
180 VARICK
13TH FLOOR
NEW YORK, N.Y. 10014
(212) 807 6777
212-807-6111
212-807-8999 FAX
Web Site: www.qmodels.com

REQUEST MODEL MANAGEMENT
119 West 22nd St Second Floor
NY, NY 10011
Phone: (212) 924-4241
Website: http://www.requestmodels.com

R&L MODEL MANAGEMENT
203 W. 23 St. Suite 400
NEW YORK, NY 10011
Phone: (212) 935-2300
Web Site: http://r-lmodels.com

THE STONED MODELING AGENCY
5 OAKDALE MANOR # B-15
SUFFERN, NY 10901
Phone: (914) 368 1625
Web Site: http://www.fashioncentral.net

UNIVERSITY MODELS INC.
15 PLEASANTVILLE ROAD
OSSINING, NY 10562
Phone: 1-877-4-UMODEL
Website: http://www.umodels.com

WILHELMINA MODELS INC
300 S PARK AVE # 2
NEW YORK, NY 10010
Phone: (212) 473-0700
Fax: (212) 473-3223
Web Site: http://www.wilhelmina.com

WILHELMINA RUNWAY DIV
300 S PARK AVE # 2
NEW YORK, NY 10010
Phone: (212) 473-4312

WOMEN MODEL MANAGEMENT
199 LAFAYETTE ST
NEW YORK, NY 10012
Phone: (212) 334-7480
Fax: (212) 334-7492

ZOLI MANAGEMENT INC
3 W 18TH ST
NEW YORK, NY 10011
Phone: (212) 242-1500
Fax: (212) 242-7505

FFT
381 Park Avenue South # 821
NY, NY 10016
Phone: 212-686-4343
http://www.fftmodels.com
fft@fftmodels.com

CED
257 Park Avenue South # 900/950
NY, NY 10010
Phone: 212-477-1666
http://www.cedtalent.com
info@cedtalent.com

The reason why I chose to only to put agencies that are in New York City is simple. New York City is the modeling capital of the world everyone who is anyone is in the big apple. All the big agencies are there if you're going to be successful it's going to be in New York!

You will need an introduction letter that you will enclose with your comp card to see if they are interested in representing you, very important include a self addressed stamp envelope when you send your comp card, two reason one you will need to keep the cost of your comp card at a minimum, two you will want to know for sure that someone at the agency got the card looked at it a was not interested in your look and mail the comp card back. Always direct your snapshots to the "New Faces division", these talented agents specialize in reviewing amateur snapshots and they will contact you for an interview.

<u>Below is a sample letter:</u>

PJ MEDINA
124 ANYWHERE STREET
NEW YORK N.Y. 11220

April 1,2005
To: New Face Department or commercial department
Dear Sir or madam:

My name is Pj medina and I am very interested in becoming a model. I am 20 years old 6'0" tall I weigh 160 pounds, I am a 40 jacket and a size 12 shoe my eyes and hair are brown.

I reside in Brooklyn New York. I work as a receptionist for Bally's. Please contact me and let me know if you think I have what it takes to be a model and if you would be interested in representing me.

If not, I would appreciate any advice on how I can improve myself or any suggestion of other agencies that might be interested in my look.

I am enclosing my comp card and a self addressed, stamped envelope. I would really appreciate it if could return my comp card and any advice or comments.

Thank you
Sincerely yours,

Now, you will have to became proactive 3 weeks after you have send the com cards with your intro letter if you have not landed an agent your going to pick up the phone and call the agency if your not in New York just go on line and run a modeling agency search.

Some agencies hold open calls frequently call the agencies to confirm if you will need an appointment, or can you just show up, ask time, date and location of the open call. Open calls are a version of an open house were anyone who is interest in breaking into modeling is free to drop in during the open call and meet a booker or agent. Go on as many open calls as you because can they're a great experience and a learning tool. Even if 12 agencies say no the 13 might say yes.

Scam alert

From time to time you will come across people calming to be with an entertainment group or a scout for an entertainment group calming that their company can help you land an agent all you have to do is sign an agreement with them. Look at a sample of one of these agreements I came across and see if you can find out what's wrong with this one.

THE ANYMORE ENTERTAINMENT GROUP

"WORKING AGREEMENT"

This us a working agreement between The Anymore Entertainment Group and ____you_____. This agreement states that the undersigned will appear on the following date _____

To perform or provide the following service modeling. In the event that Anymore needs ongoing services provided by You/your Company this agreement will be active for a period of on year; Anymore will be responsible for providing auditions for the length of this binding agreement. Anymore is responsible for providing no less than five auditions over the period that this agreement is active. Any jobs secured as a result of referrals made by made by Anymore Entertainment Group, you will be assessed a 20% charge, from the final negotiated amount for the contract. This working agreement is not exclusive, in that, you are able to find and secure jobs on your own, as long as they do not interfere with your working agreement with anymore. Should a conflict of interest arise, be advised that Anymore reserves the right to terminate this agreement at will.

Sign_____

Well what do you think?

Let me tell you what I think!

1) Modeling is not entertainment, it is work
2) Your locked in for a year
3) Anymore Entertainment is responsible for 5 auditions, their can pull that out of a newspaper or online
4) Anymore Entertainment gets 20% of your money weather they get you the job or not the industries standard is 10% that is the law in New York State why should Anyone Entertainment get paid for work they did not get you?
5) Anyone Entertainment can terminate you or break this agreement at anytime but you can't.

Do not assume strangers who call themselves model scouts are legitimists. Ask for a business card. A business card does not prove anything but it is a start. There are bogus model scouts who falsely claim to represent top agencies, but when those agencies are called, they deny ever hearing of them.

So forever one model working today that got there start with a scout, 98 of them got scammed. Most legitimate agencies never advertise in the newspaper, they will be listed in the yellow page or online.

STEP SIX

Booking Whom?

UNDERSTANDING YOUR BODY, HEATH AND WELLNESS.

Take your vitamins

A vitamin every day: It is very difficult to satisfy the recommended daily allowance (RDA) of vitamins and minerals without supplementation. Many scientific studies have validated the benefits of taking a daily multivitamin and mineral formulation. There are many supplement varieties on the market. This will help ensure that the necessary proteins, fats and enzymes are present for enhanced and efficient uptake for use by your body.

It is very important for a model that wants to take more responsibility for his or her own health to do the necessary homework and choose what is right for him or her. You can also discuss this with your physician and have them help you choose what is appropriate for your needs. Here are some beauty tips that are guaranteed to work, if you follow them all. There is no point eating fresh fruit and vegetables, and then smoking like a chimney! Here are some tips for you;

1. Floss your teeth
2. Eat Good Food.
3. Sleep. At least eight hours. A good night's kip will make you look years younger.

4. Don't Smoke.
5. Don't Drink Alcohol.
6. Don't Sunbathe.
7. Drink lots of water 8-12 glasses a day.
8. Exfoliate your face daily with a facial scrub it will gently remove dull surface cells to reveal a Smoother skin.
9. Don't Wear a Beard or Moustache, Or Long Hair (for men).
10. Don't Have Cosmetic Surgery.
11. Don't Over-diet, Over-exercise.

Let talk for a few minutes about money again. I need you to think about this for just a few minutes and what I'm about to tell you are actual facts. Did you know that most of all the money in the world is in the hands of about ten percent of the population. Why am I telling you this, you may be asking?

The reason is simple I want to change your perception of money. We are coming towards the end of this book and the last thing you need to be doing is worrying about money so I'm going to ask you to stop doing it, stop worrying about your lack of money.

Why is it that so many people worry about money? Do you know that wealthy people never worry about money; they worry about making it.

The focus is always on the processes.

They have so much love for the processes of making money that they never think or say I can't afford this or that. Instead the thought process is I need to find the next audition so that I can buy this and that.

Why is it that so many people feel so bad about money? It's because of negative beliefs about money from when you and I were little children, handed down by our parents and now they're in our subconscious mine.

Thing like what do you think I am made of money, we can't afford that, we have no money, do you think money grows on trees and my all time favorite do I look like a ATM to you? When we are little children we believe just about everything we are told. So without realizing it, we grow up into adulthood with all these negative beliefs.

Now you know that none of those things where true.

> *"When you realize there is nothing lacking, the whole world belongs to you"*
>
> Laozi founder of Taoism

October 2003 will be a time I will never forget. My financial life seemed to be in ruins.

That year I lost my job after seven years of service.

Having partied all my saving away in the early part of 2003 I found myself without a job, no money and no way to pay any bills even my rent was behind. To make matter worse the job market was terrible. It was the worst time in my life.

Moving into my best friend apartment and sleeping on his sofa for the next 90-day, what a lesson in humility. I had hit rock bottom and the thing about hitting rock bottom is you have no here to go but up and that's what I did.

Here is a side note all of my so called other friends were nowhere to be found it was as if they all just disappeared. Funny how when you're broke you find out whom your friends really are.

One day while going through classified ads looking for work, by the way something I did everyday and send out at least ten resumes per week. My good friend told me about a book I should read. Now at the risk of sounding like I'm working for the man or I'm getting some sort of kick back, which I am not.

The reason I'm telling you about this book is that I truly believe the book help change my life and maybe just maybe it can do the same for you.

The name of the book is Rich Dad Poor Dad by Robert Kiyosaki

He has dozens of books that are amazing.

STEP SIX

So you want to be in pictures

YOUR MONEY AND JOBS JUST FOR SURVIVAL.

Living in the big apple

NEW YORK is the fashion capitals of the world and most advertising companies are based in the big apple and because of this the top modeling agencies are in the city as well. This is the home of most supermodels so when walking down the street does not be surprised to see two or three a day. But living in Gotham city cost lots of money. Trust me, I know its costly to live in New York City I have been doing it for most of my life but for you the up and coming model, I am going to share with you a few tips I have learned along the way.

Lets start with an apartment. But you need to keep in mind the rule of 25. Living in Manhattan will set you back anywhere from 40% to 50% of your income so why not look towards the outer borough such Brooklyn, Queens, the Bronx, or Staten Island because the rent is much less and if your dead set in living in Manhattan, try upper Manhattan like Harlem, Hamilton Heights, or Washington Heights. It may not be beautiful but it is a lot cheaper. I also strongly recommend that you get a roommate or two if the apartment is big. This will bring down the cost. If you're new in town odds are you do not know anyone who is looking for a roommate, well help is just a click away. www.easyroommate.com and it's free. Find one.

Eating in New York can burn a hole in your pocket to.

Try not to eat out as much maybe brown paper bag lunch and stay away from star bucks and fancy or trendy restaurants try to budget yourself to spending $100.00 a month on food. Instated find a nice ethnic cubbyhole supermarket that's clean and uses a shopping list and stick to it. And maybe get a loyalty card. Getting around in NEW YORK

Just leave the car home the subway is the fastest, most reliable and it is cheap to! The cost in 2005 was $2.00 a ride but for $75.00 a month you can ride all day and as many time you need. Its called a monthly metro-card and it's great. Most subway lines run 24 hours a day. The Staten Island ferry is free. And although crime is down always try to travel by day or if traveling at night bring a friend along.

Saving some coins in New York City.

There's a bank on every block so focus on finding one that offers free stuff. Like free checking or saving and most are open seven days a week, so find one that suits you.

The city that never sleeps, They don't call NEW YORK that for nothing, its true the big apple is a party town from Broadway, to night club, to the best restaurants, this town has the best and its open 24 hours a day 7 days a week. Beware, you'll be broke in a week. Enjoy the city slowly and do things that are not so costly (there is so much to do that is free.) Go to a newsstand and pickup timeout magazine its put out weekly and it's full of stuff to do in the city that's FREE!!

SO GO OUT ENJOY THE GREATEST CITY IN THE WORLD

STEP SEVEN

GETTING THE JOB, MAKING THE MONEY LET THE GAMES BEGIN

STEP SEVEN

Getting the job, getting the money let the games begin

CHANGING THE WAY YOU THINK.

He, who has an amazing life, imagines what he loves and wants he feels it as if it is real and as if like magic it appears in his life.

I want to talk with you about the power of your imagination. You can truly be, do and have anything your heart desires. If you can dream it you can do it. History has shown us the countless number of humans who have done the unimaginable and all they had was a dream. It is my opinion that the biggest names in Hollywood today started with just a dream and used that dream to become the biggest name in the business

They didn't know how, but they knew that someway, somehow they where going to make it. I am grooming you to do the same in this step.

I want you just for a moment to dream with me about what is possible and I want you to understand, if you imagine it you can live it in reality. I want to talk to you about the power of you imagination. The power of the human imagination has been talked about and written about for decades.

For now I want you to focus your attention to acting and how if you can imagine yourself as a successful actor and doing the things actor say and do you can live it. It will come into your life.

This is what I would like for you to do. Everyday for the next ninety days we are going to play a game and these are the rules of our game.

Before leaving your home to start your day your going to spend ten minutes standing by the door that leads to the outside of your home with your eye's closed and your going to start to imagine and I want you to try to imagine in detail and in color, even in 3-D well you get my point.

What would your life be like if you were a successful actor. See yourself being at a movie set or in a television commercial or even at the red carpet promoting your newest film. Smell it, taste it and touch it in your imagination's eye.

Secondly open the door and exit the home and start acting as if. As if you are that person in your imagination. How would you walk, how would you talk, where would you eat lunch.

Start acting as if now start living the life you where meant to live. Your dream will become your reality. ***Start now!***

STEP SEVEN

Getting the job, getting the money let the games begin

TIME MANAGEMENT THE ABILITY TO MANAGE YOURSELF.

It's time to shine and prove they made the right choice.

Now that I've gotten that out of the way, congratulations!! Your hard work has paid off. From this moment on your life will never be the same, if you continue to apply what you've learned and continue to be grateful for all the things your receiving no matter now big or small and just focus on managing your time and yourself you will win at this game.

Understand that when opportunity collides with preparation, this equals success.

And this is what we have been doing throughout this book, preparing you for this moment in time. So don't blow it! So do your homework, be fresh and get there thirty minutes early. Get a good night sleep. You can celebrate later.

STEP SEVEN

Getting the job, getting the money let the games begin

GETTING DOWN TO THE FUNDAMENTALS OF THE BUSINESS, I MEAN MODELING BUSINESS.

The average career span of a Model is till about age 21, for females males till about forty with that being said you need to have a back up plan and I will tell you that your future can be amazing. Modeling opens so many doors for the person who remains humble and focused. It is a natural transition to go from Modeling to acting and with so many actors today coming from the modeling world that if you hold anyone that your ultimate goal was to become a famous actor no one would be surprise or even a recording artists.

And in the world of entertainment it's not what you know, it's whom you know.

If that is your ultimate goal to become an actor at some point and make millions of dollar, traveling the world on movies set and walking the red carpet my I suggest my newest book Acting As Your Job.

STEP SEVEN

Getting the job, getting the money let the games begin

YOUR MONEY AND JOBS JUST FOR SURVIVAL.

PAYING THE RENT

While pursuing your dream of modeling you are going to need money to pay the rent, eat and pay bills. You may be thinking, "well I have a job but is that going to allow me the freedom to go on go and see's or will it slow me down".

Bear in mind the 90% of all photo shoots, go and sees, are done in the day anywhere between the hours of 7 am and 7 pm so you're going to need to be free within this time frame. The trick then is finding a job or a temperate job that allows you to be fixable with your work hours so that you can run around and go on go and see's and photo shoots. If you are serious about modeling you are going to supplement your income.

We like to call these survival jobs

Temping most temp agencies are thrilled to have an enthusiastic, skilled employee and are willing to give a little time off and flexibility in order to keep that employee on staff as long as the employee is professional, punctual, and willing to give plenty of notice when he or she is unavailable for work due to a photo shoot or go and see.

Teaching If academic work is your cup of tea but you do not like the idea of a full day with many students; you want to get registered with a tutorial service. There are several companies that do SAT—prep and straight-out academic tutoring all over town providing excellent pay and great flexibility.

Fitness trainer becoming a certified fitness trainer is also a very good idea they make their own hours based on their free time and make at least $20.00 an hour per client, there are so many gym's in New York City who are always looking for new trainers.

SEAT FILLER Another fun job is filling seats at awards shows. The pay is good and your meet all kinds of cool people. Seatfiller.com is the site you to sign up. Go ahead and give it a shot

There are so many more model friendly jobs out there you and just need to look. The best place to start looking is at all the listing at entertainmentcareers.net you'll thank me.

And as always best of luck, now get to work.

I am aware that gratitude is the greatest amplifier of life; I say to you I am truly GRATEFUL to you for purchasing this book.

Pj Medina